when WHAT gives way to WHY

The Companion Workbook

Rebecca Claeys

Author: Claeys, Rebecca
Title: When What Gives Way to Why The Companion Workbook
ISBN: 979-8-9890352-2-9

Cover Design: Brenay Torres
Cover Art: Sanna Nilsson
Photography Credit: Maeve Turner-Johnson

Reddig Relationship Circles Model © 2022 Jennifer Reddig, MSW, LICSW, CCTP
Used with permission

The Phoenix and Leaf logo is a trademark of Cleopatra's Seeds, LLC

Published by Cleopatra's Seeds, LLC
Spring Green, WI
www.cleopatrasseeds.com

TABLE OF CONTENTS

How To Use This Workbook

This workbook was crafted to be a companion to my book, **When What Gives Way to Why**. The book contains 13 exercises to help you work through the transformational journey that is my signature Soul Alchemy Cycle. Through this journey, you will learn to deconstruct what you think you know, purify your language around it, transmute your beliefs, and rebuild your reality.

This will provide you with the foundational infrastructure to find your way out of burnout (or avoid falling into it in the first place) and buffer yourself from falling back in. No more spirals of fatigue and hopelessness here! You have, at your fingertips, tools specifically designed to help you step into real healing and define *your* success on *your* terms.

The exercises here align with the exercises in the book. In some cases, I've created extra prompts or ways of thinking about the exercise material and included it here. My hope is that it will help you move through this work so you can find the healing you deserve.

Many of the exercises include templates. I couldn't fill this book as full of workspace as I wanted to, or the workbook would have ended up being longer than the book! Instead, I've shared a decent amount of space to start working and provided blank templates in an appendix in the back. I recommend using the appendix as a master to make copies from if you need more. Several, but not all, of the templates are available on my website to be printed, too.

So, dig in! There's no time like the present to invest in your healing. Remember, you're never alone on this journey. I'm with you every step of the way, and I can't wait to see you at the finish line.

Rebecca

deconstruct

nigredo

Be willing, throughout this process and throughout your life, to unpot yourself.

Exercise 1: Creature Comforts

Answer the following questions to fill your personalized gardening bag with tools for nurturing yourself when you're moving through uncomfortable spaces. There is room at the end to fill in your own questions and answers if you think of any as you work through this exercise.

What makes you feel alive?

_____

_____

_____

_____

When you are hurting, do you need social connection to heal, or do you prefer to keep to yourself?

_____

_____

_____

Are you somewhere in between?

_____

_____

Are there certain people that recharge you and others who drain you?

_____

_____

_____

What is your favorite scent?

_____

_____

_____

What scent(s) do you need to avoid?

_____

_____

_____

What food makes you feel energized, ready to conquer the world?

_____

_____

_____

_____

Do you need movement to feel like yourself?

_____

_____

_____

What kind?

_____

_____

What intensity?

_____

_____

If you had a week with no responsibilities and no budget limits, what would you do?

_____

_____

_____

_____

_____

Where would you go, and who would you visit or take with you?

_____

_____

_____

_____

Does music soothe your mind, energize you, or irritate you?

_____

_____

_____

How do different types of music impact your mood and how your body feels?

_____

_____

_____

What textures feel good on your skin?

_____

_____

_____

What textures do you need to avoid at all costs?

_____

_____

_____

Additional Questions/Answers

_____

_____

_____

_____

_____

_____

_____

_____

Your village consists of the people you trust with the most intimate, vulnerable pieces of you.

Exercise 2: Find Your Village

Use this model, created by Jennifer Reddig, MSW, LICSW, CCTP, as a guide for finding your village. The following pages contain blank versions of the model for you to use. Feel free to draw additional circles as makes sense for your village.

Remember as you work through this exercise that where someone lands on the model is controlled by their behavior toward you, positive or negative. Nobody inherently gets a specific place on the map because of a role they hold. This map is for you and you alone; be honest in your assessment of these relationships.

Also remember that children do not belong on this model. We cannot expect them to hold space for us as we would an adult. You can love them very much, with your whole being, and it is kindest for both you and them to leave them off your map.

There is an additional blank model in the Template Appendix at the back of this workbook.

©2022 J. Reddig, MSW, LICSW

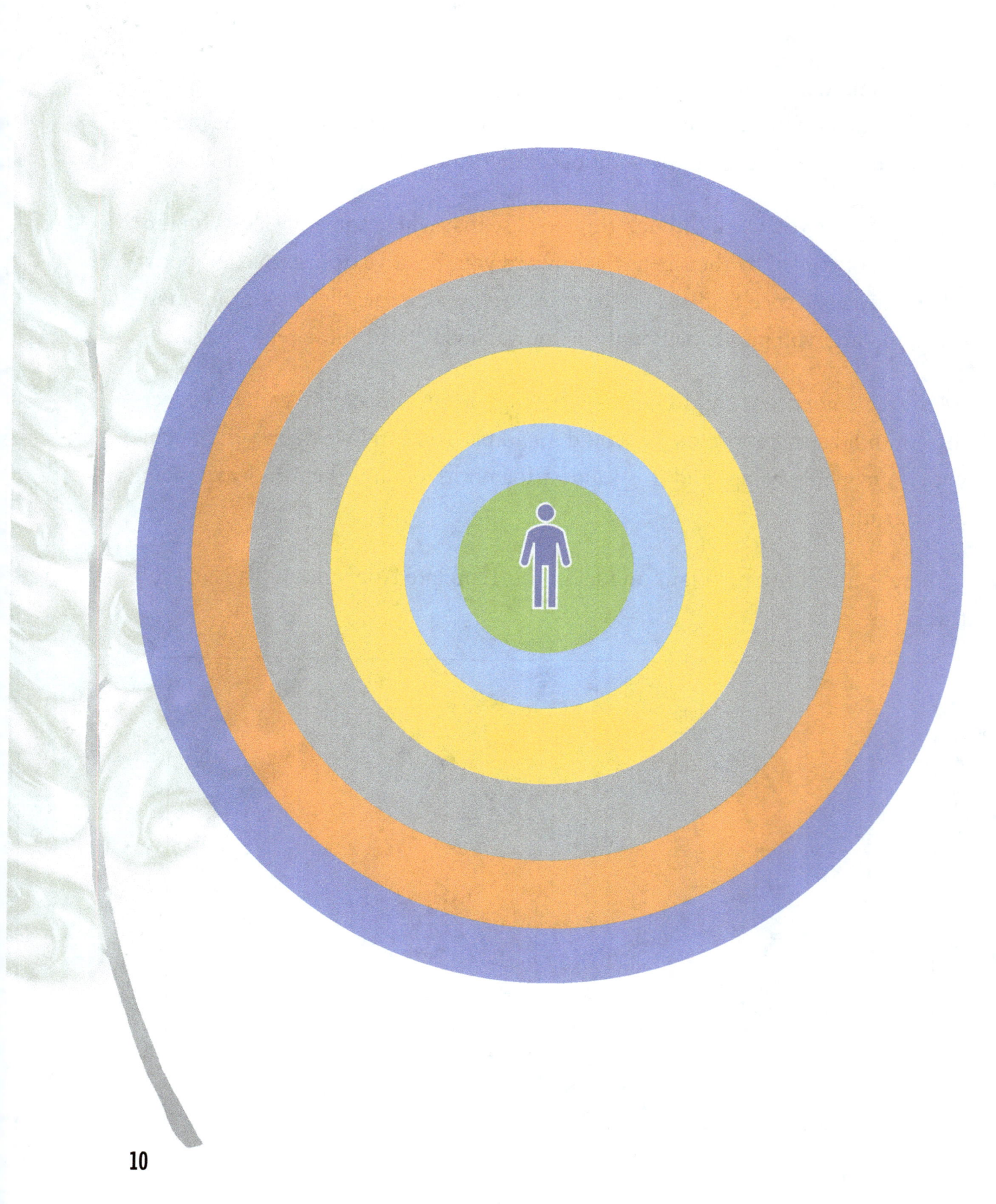

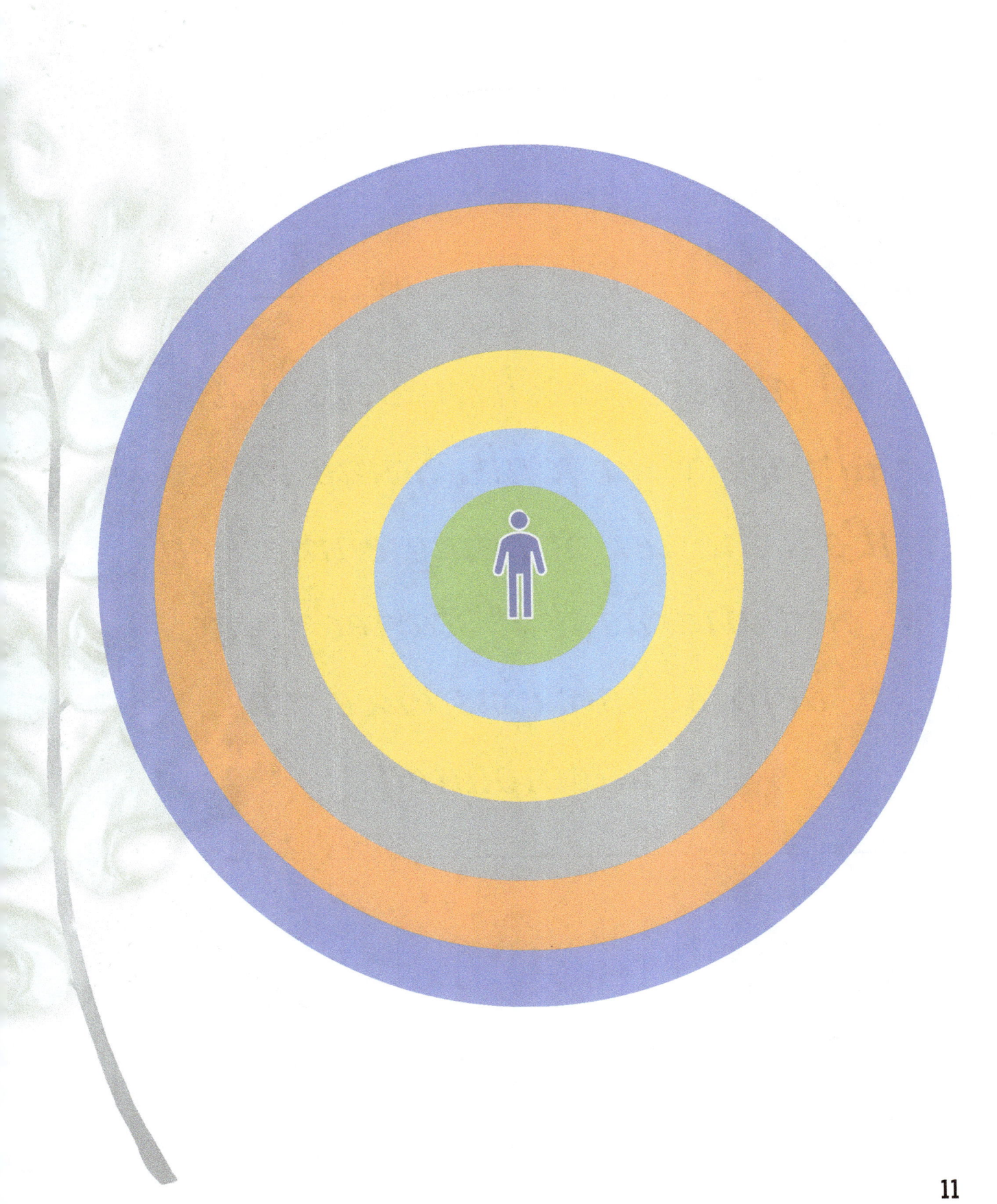

11

I'm here to tell you it's not always your fault. Sometimes, it's a matter of being enmeshed in patterns that started long before your existence was contemplated.

Exercise 3: Releasing the Burden

Use the following template to name and explore three things you feel responsible for fixing.

I feel responsible for fixing

_____

_____

because

_____

_____

Does it keep you up at night or distract from your work?

_____

Are you blaming yourself for this situation existing in the first place?

_____

If so, what does the voice say to you when you blame yourself?

_____

_____

Is it true?

_____

Whose voice is it? Is it actually yours, or is it someone else's that you've internalized?

_____

_____

What power does this thing hold over you?

_____

_____

Who gave it that power?

_____

Is it valid?

_____

Is this situation yours to manage or does it belong elsewhere?

_____

Is there action you need to take?

_____

_____

Can you release it?

_____

I feel responsible for fixing

_____

_____

because

_____

_____

Does it keep you up at night or distract from your work?

_____

Are you blaming yourself for this situation existing in the first place?

_____

If so, what does the voice say to you when you blame yourself?

_____

_____

Is it true?

_____

Whose voice is it? Is it actually yours, or is it someone else's that you've internalized?

_____

_____

What power does this thing hold over you?

_____

_____

Who gave it that power?

_____

Is it valid?

_____

Is this situation yours to manage or does it belong elsewhere?

_____

Is there action you need to take?

_____

_____

Can you release it?

_____

I feel responsible for fixing

_____

_____

because

_____

_____

Does it keep you up at night or distract from your work?

_____

Are you blaming yourself for this situation existing in the first place?

_____

If so, what does the voice say to you when you blame yourself?

_____

_____

Is it true?

_____

Whose voice is it? Is it actually yours, or is it someone else's that you've internalized?

_____

_____

What power does this thing hold over you?

_____

_____

Who gave it that power?

_____

Is it valid?

_____

Is this situation yours to manage or does it belong elsewhere?

_____

Is there action you need to take?

_____

_____

Can you release it?

_____

Your responsibility is absolutely to take action from here forward, and you don't need to be carrying responsibility that isn't yours. Place it on the ground and walk away with your head held high.

You can't hold onto the myth of productivity and avoid burnout. You have to release it to create space for your new understanding of yourself and the world around you.

Exercise 4: Letting Go

Set a timer for 15 minutes for this exercise. Answer instinctively; don't overthink your response. Remember that there are no right or wrong answers in these exercises. This is about you, where you're at, and where you're moving toward.

As you progress through the following questions, note first what your answer was when you read through the prompts in Chapter 1. Then, review the prompt again through the lens of releasing the idea that you must always be productive and note down your answers.

How would you spend your time if you had no obligations and money was no object?

_____

_____

_____

How would your day flow in this world you've built?

_____

_____

_____

Your week?

_____

_____

Your year?

_____

_____

Is it your instinct to plan things to accomplish or ways of existing? Why?

_____

_____

_____

If it's a mix of the two, which is weighted more heavily? Why?

_____

_____

Would your answer bring you to a place of peace and contentment?

_____

_____

Would you regret your answer after living in it for a year?

_____

_____

_____

Five years?

_____

_____

_____

Ten years?

_____

_____

_____

Did your answers change from your old way of thinking? How?

_____

_____

_____

What emotions went through you as you looked at these questions from a new perspective?

_____

_____

_____

purify
albedo

We intentionally get uncomfortable - we unpot ourselves on the regular - and we do hard things!

Exercise 5: Spring Cleaning

Spend about 20 minutes going through these prompts. Respond instinctively; don't spend too long thinking about your answers.

What did you want to be when you grew up at age:

5?

_____

9?

_____

14?

_____

18?

_____

25?

_____

What influenced the changes between each age?

_____

_____

Were you introduced to new ideas?

_____

_____

_____

_____

Did you feel pressure to move away from something? If so, what kind?

_____

_____

_____

_____

Where did that pressure come from?

_____

_____

_____

What pressures were most influential?

_____

_____

If you could choose anything to do now, without restriction on money/time/ education (assume you have plenty of all of them for the rest of your life), what would you do?

_____

_____

_____

_____

Is your choice creative or productive?

_____

_____

Why do you lean the way you do?

_____

_____

Does thinking about this bring up any emotions? If so, what kinds?

_____

_____

_____

Where and when did you first start feeling those emotions around how you move through the world?

_____

_____

_____

_____

_____

What parts of your answers are based in reality?

_____

_____

_____

_____

What have you been told that keeps you focused on a *what* rather than leaning into your *why*?

_____

_____

_____

_____

As it turns out, that curiosity I was born with and wielded so naturally as a child is an incredibly powerful tool.

transmute

citrinitas

You're trying to discover your core self; make sure that core self has space to speak.

Exercise 6: Field Notes

Fill in the Description column of the table below with items, events, or people you identify as Personal Artifacts, Things that Bring You Joy, Things that Bring You Pride, Things that Bring You Peace, or Your Village – Extended Edition.

As much as possible, move through one component at a time and catalog as much as you can. If you happen on something that belongs later, that's ok, put it in your notes in line with whatever you're cataloging. An unnumbered table is in the Template Appendix at the back of this workbook for more space.

Leave the last two columns of the table blank for now; you'll come back to them with work from other exercises later.

Artifact No.	Description	Words/Ideas	Values
1			
2			
3			
4			
5			

Artifact No.	Description	Words/Ideas	Values
6			
7			
8			
9			
10			
11			
12			
13			
14			
15			
16			

Artifact No.	Description	Words/Ideas	Values
17			
18			
19			
20			
21			
22			
23			
24			
25			
26			
27			

Breathe. Look closely – what's missing from the picture? If it doesn't make sense, tear it out and try again. Don't be afraid of tearing things out.

Exercise 7: Investigation

Fill in the template on the following pages to explore why each item in your field notes was worthy of inclusion.

- As with your field notes, stick with one component as much as possible during this investigation phase. As a reminder, those components are:

  - Personal Artifacts

  - Things that Bring You Joy

  - Things that Bring You Pride

  - Things that Bring You Peace

  - Your Village – Extended Edition

- Use one log page per artifact, adding more as needed. You can find in a blank copy of this template on my website or in the Template Appendix at the back of this workbook if you need more.

- Don't overthink your answers here. Trust your instincts and write whatever comes to mind first. There are no right or wrong answers, and the only person this needs to make sense to is you. Shed the should!

- When you have completed investigating all of your artifacts, go back to your table from Exercise 6 (page 35) and fill in the 'Words/Ideas' column with your answers to the final question on each template page.

_____

_____

_____

Is this artifact connected to a person, event, or both? Describe the significance of this below.

_____

_____

What emotions are tied to the artifact itself?

_____

_____

What emotions are tied to the people or events connected to this artifact?

_____

_____

What two words/ideas come to mind first when you think about this artifact in totality?

_____

_____

_____

_____

_____

Is this artifact connected to a person, event, or both? Describe the significance of this below.

_____

_____

What emotions are tied to the artifact itself?

_____

_____

What emotions are tied to the people or events connected to this artifact?

_____

_____

What two words/ideas come to mind first when you think about this artifact in totality?

_____

_____

_____

_____

_____

Is this artifact connected to a person, event, or both? Describe the significance of this below.

_____

_____

What emotions are tied to the artifact itself?

_____

_____

What emotions are tied to the people or events connected to this artifact?

_____

_____

What two words/ideas come to mind first when you think about this artifact in totality?

_____

_____

_____

_____

_____

Is this artifact connected to a person, event, or both? Describe the significance of this below.

_____

_____

What emotions are tied to the artifact itself?

_____

_____

What emotions are tied to the people or events connected to this artifact?

_____

_____

What two words/ideas come to mind first when you think about this artifact in totality?

_____

_____

_____

_____

_____

Is this artifact connected to a person, event, or both? Describe the significance of this below.

_____

_____

What emotions are tied to the artifact itself?

_____

_____

What emotions are tied to the people or events connected to this artifact?

_____

_____

What two words/ideas come to mind first when you think about this artifact in totality?

_____

_____

_____

_____

_____

Is this artifact connected to a person, event, or both? Describe the significance of this below.

_____

_____

What emotions are tied to the artifact itself?

_____

_____

What emotions are tied to the people or events connected to this artifact?

_____

_____

What two words/ideas come to mind first when you think about this artifact in totality?

_____

_____

_____

_____

_____

Is this artifact connected to a person, event, or both? Describe the significance of this below.

_____

_____

What emotions are tied to the artifact itself?

_____

_____

What emotions are tied to the people or events connected to this artifact?

_____

_____

What two words/ideas come to mind first when you think about this artifact in totality?

_____

_____

_____

_____

_____

Is this artifact connected to a person, event, or both? Describe the significance of this below.

_____

_____

What emotions are tied to the artifact itself?

_____

_____

What emotions are tied to the people or events connected to this artifact?

_____

_____

What two words/ideas come to mind first when you think about this artifact in totality?

_____

_____

_____

_____

_____

Is this artifact connected to a person, event, or both? Describe the significance of this below.

_____

_____

What emotions are tied to the artifact itself?

_____

_____

What emotions are tied to the people or events connected to this artifact?

_____

_____

What two words/ideas come to mind first when you think about this artifact in totality?

_____

_____

_____

_____

_____

Is this artifact connected to a person, event, or both? Describe the significance of this below.

_____

_____

What emotions are tied to the artifact itself?

_____

_____

What emotions are tied to the people or events connected to this artifact?

_____

_____

What two words/ideas come to mind first when you think about this artifact in totality?

_____

_____

_____

_____

_____

Is this artifact connected to a person, event, or both? Describe the significance of this below.

_____

_____

What emotions are tied to the artifact itself?

_____

_____

What emotions are tied to the people or events connected to this artifact?

_____

_____

What two words/ideas come to mind first when you think about this artifact in totality?

_____

_____

_____

_____

_____

Is this artifact connected to a person, event, or both? Describe the significance of this below.

_____

_____

What emotions are tied to the artifact itself?

_____

_____

What emotions are tied to the people or events connected to this artifact?

_____

_____

What two words/ideas come to mind first when you think about this artifact in totality?

_____

_____

_____

_____

_____

Is this artifact connected to a person, event, or both? Describe the significance of this below.

_____

_____

What emotions are tied to the artifact itself?

_____

_____

What emotions are tied to the people or events connected to this artifact?

_____

_____

What two words/ideas come to mind first when you think about this artifact in totality?

_____

_____

You are so very close to knowing who your core self is and what your purpose is! You are holding the keys to your success in these lists.

You're tapping into your core self here; listen to it and hear what it's trying to tell you.

Exercise 8: Analysis

The following pages contain blank shapes that you can use to organize your words from Exercise 7. These are the same words in the third column of your chart from Exercise 6 (page 35).

If you have a word appear more than once, that's ok! It means it's especially important to you. Only create one shape per word, though. You may want to denote those important words with a mark of your choice on the shape piece.

Use the small shapes for the words in your chart. Use the large shapes for category labels as you identify them. Cut the shapes out and move them around to see how they fit together. Keep moving them around until it feels right.

Yes, that means you should cut them out of the workbook. Get tactile with this exercise! Moving things around will help make the connections click more easily. Don't worry, there's a blank copy of each set in the Template Appendix so you can make copies of them later if you need to (or if you need more shapes now). You can also print them from the free .pdf worksheet on my website.

When your clusters of words are ready and you have your central thread, theme, or category labels for each, go back to your table from Exercise 6 and fill in the 'Values' column with the corresponding labels. If you have bridging words, enter all of the associated labels.

57

The process you are going through right now is mapping your core self. You're learning the values that are most important to you and giving names to them.

Exercise 9: Distillation

Step 1:

Once you've worked through mapping, review the themes that rose to the top while you were naming your categories. These are the words that you wrote in the fourth column of your chart from Exercise 6 (page 35).

What jumps out at you?

_____

_____

_____

_____

_____

_____

_____

_____

_____

_____

_____

Can you distill them down further? Aim for three to five, and there's no limit.

_____

_____

_____

_____

_____

_____

_____

My core self's values are:

_____

_____

_____

_____

_____

_____

Your themes are your core self's values. Absent all other roles you have taken on in your life, these are the things that are most important to the one and only you.

What is most important is that when you have crafted it, the words sit right with your spirit and flow easily from your lips. You can speak it into a mirror, explain it, and say, "This is my purpose. This describes my core self. It is who I am."

Exercise 10: Naming Your Why

I recommend you sit with your values to complete this task. Take some time to yourself. Grab a cup of coffee, tea, or whatever makes you feel warm and full. Get comfortable. Pamper yourself for a bit. Some light background noise is ok, though silence heavily encourages you to be centered and mindful of your thoughts.

Stew on these words - the themes, threads, and values you identified in Exercise 9.

How do they connect to how you have lived your life?

_____

_____

_____

_____

How do you want them to connect to your life?

_____

_____

_____

_____

_____

Use the space on these two pages to write out words or phrases that could become your purpose statement. Workshop it here until it feels easy.

rebuild

rubedo

You need a space that is exclusively yours to do this work in. You'll need it as you consult your map throughout your travels, too.

Exercise 11: Haven Sweet Haven

Step 1:

What space or spaces are good candidates for you to claim for yourself?

_____

_____

_____

_____

_____

_____

What are some potential barriers to keeping this space sacred as your very own?

_____

_____

_____

_____

_____

_____

Step 2:

What boundaries, physical and/or verbal, can you place to reinforce each of these as your sacred space?

_____

_____

_____

_____

_____

Given these reflections, which space is the best choice for you?

_____

_____

_____

With whom will you need to be firmest about these boundaries?

_____

_____

_____

_____

What cues can you give them to look for when you are not to be disturbed or, conversely, when you are open to having them join you in your space?

_____

_____

_____

_____

_____

_____

Step 3:

Which of your personal artifacts that you identified in your table from Exercise 6 (page 35) speak most strongly to your purpose? Where in your space do they belong?

_____

_____

_____

_____

_____

Crafting a Purpose Board

Begin by writing out your purpose statement and/or the values behind it. Include these words on the board as a visual connection to your core self.

_____

_____

_____

_____

What images connect you to those words? Are there places or people that belong on your purpose board? Look back to your table from Exercise 6 for ideas.

_____

_____

_____

_____

_____

_____

_____

Color plays an important role in evoking memories and creating connections. How can you add color to your board to facilitate that connection?

_____

_____

_____

_____

_____

Where in your sacred space does your purpose board belong? Where will it be most helpful in reminding you of your *why* and helping you *shed the should*?

_____

_____

_____

_____

_____

_____

_____

This is a pattern, too. It might feel impossible at first glance, and the pattern is right there, waiting for you to click into it.

Exercise 12: Your Personal Treasure Map

The following pages will guide you through all five steps of Exercise 12.

As you work through the steps, keep an extra watchful eye out for 'shoulds' creeping into your process. Approach this part of your work like an anthropologist, with curiosity and without judgment.

Step 1: Inventory

The next two pages contain a table to begin an inventory of your learned identities, similar to how you created your Field Notes inventory table in Exercise 6 (page 35). This time, though, you'll fill out all columns in the chart right away.

Remember that learned identities are roles you were socialized into that define your relationship to someone else, like spouse, parent, coworker, friend, etc. You contain multitudes of these, so start with the easy ones that relate to your work life, your family life, and your social life.

Use one row per learned identity. Name it and identify what environment(s) it shows up in, who it's in relation to, and whether/which social restrictions apply.

Also, start to think about how these identities overlap when you're in a situation where more than one applies. Which restrictions take precedence? Why?

Learned Identity Name	Primary Environment	Interacts with (People)	Behavior?	Restricted in: Language?	Dress?

Learned Identity Name	Primary Environment	Interacts with (People)	Restricted in:		
			Behavior?	Language?	Dress?

Learned Identity Name	Primary Environment	Interacts with (People)	Restricted in: Behavior?	Restricted in: Language?	Restricted in: Dress?

Learned Identity Name	Primary Environment	Interacts with (People)	Restricted in:		
			Behavior?	Language?	Dress?

85

Step 2: Extrapolate

The following pages have templates for building out your rainbow layers of learned identities.

While the templates only include a single split into two identities for the next layer, there could clearly be more than one split. These pages are meant to give you an idea of how to build out your personal map. Additional copies are available for free on my website and, of course, in the Template Appendix.

You can absolutely print them off and use them in various combinations to complete your map, and you can also choose to draw your own map on a separate piece of paper, in a computer program, or however works for your mind. Remember, this is your map – it only needs to make sense to you.

Once you've finished mapping all of these identities out, don't forget to add them to the chart from Step 1 and fill out all of the columns there for each of them.

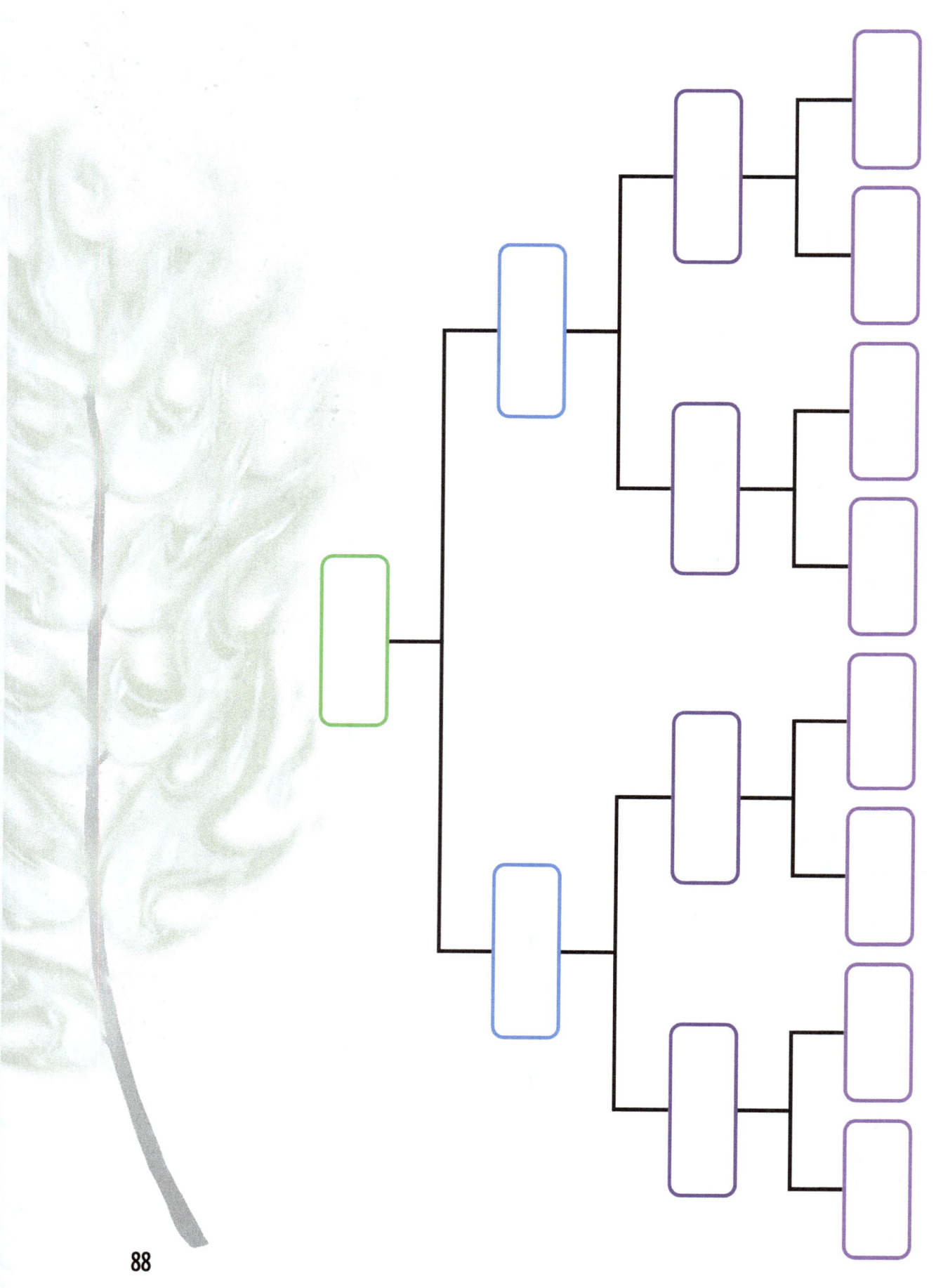

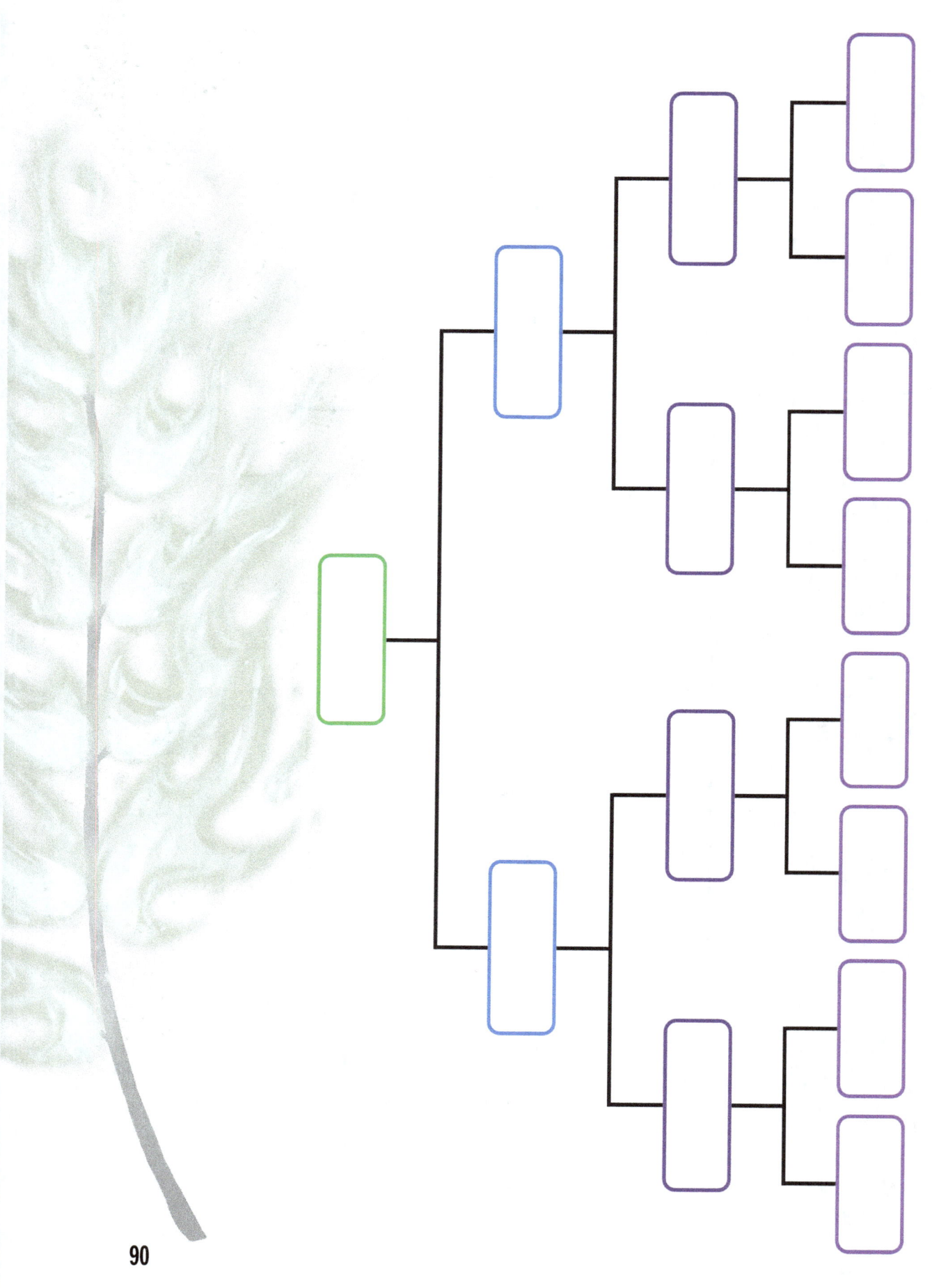

Step 3: Assess

The next page offers a template for assessing each of the learned identities you've mapped out. As you work through the template, refer back to the chart you filled out in Step 1.

Fill out one template for each learned identity on your map. It may be helpful to go down through the layers of a single red level identity at a time.

After you have completed the assessments, find the identities on your map from Step 2. Circle, highlight, or otherwise note the overall sense you get from your assessment.

For identities that are in alignment with your purpose (or mostly in alignment), mark them in green. For those that are not in alignment, mark them in red. Anything that is left – maybe they're somewhat in alignment but there are some sticking points that need to be addressed – mark them in yellow.

Learned Identity Assessment

Identity Name _____

Identity Path

Red: _____ Blue: _____

Orange: _____ Indigo: _____

Yellow: _____ Violet: _____

Green: _____ Other: _____

What about this identity aligns with your purpose?

_____

_____

_____

What about this identity does not align with your purpose?

_____

_____

_____

Is there a *what* you need to let go of? What is it?

_____

_____

Learned Identity Assessment

Identity Name _____

Identity Path

Red: _____   Blue: _____

Orange: _____   Indigo: _____

Yellow: _____   Violet: _____

Green: _____   Other: _____

What about this identity aligns with your purpose?

_____

_____

_____

What about this identity does not align with your purpose?

_____

_____

_____

Is there a *what* you need to let go of? What is it?

_____

_____

Learned Identity Assessment

Identity Name _____

Identity Path

Red: _____   Blue: _____

Orange: _____   Indigo: _____

Yellow: _____   Violet: _____

Green: _____   Other: _____

What about this identity aligns with your purpose?

_____

_____

_____

What about this identity does not align with your purpose?

_____

_____

_____

Is there a *what* you need to let go of? What is it?

_____

_____

Learned Identity Assessment

Identity Name _____

Identity Path

Red: _____   Blue: _____

Orange: _____   Indigo: _____

Yellow: _____   Violet: _____

Green: _____   Other: _____

What about this identity aligns with your purpose?

_____

_____

_____

What about this identity does not align with your purpose?

_____

_____

_____

Is there a *what* you need to let go of? What is it?

_____

_____

Learned Identity Assessment

Identity Name _____

Identity Path

Red: _____   Blue: _____

Orange: _____   Indigo: _____

Yellow: _____   Violet: _____

Green: _____   Other: _____

What about this identity aligns with your purpose?

_____

_____

_____

What about this identity does not align with your purpose?

_____

_____

_____

Is there a *what* you need to let go of? What is it?

_____

_____

Learned Identity Assessment

Identity Name _____

Identity Path

Red: _____   Blue: _____

Orange: _____   Indigo: _____

Yellow: _____   Violet: _____

Green: _____   Other: _____

What about this identity aligns with your purpose?

_____

_____

_____

What about this identity does not align with your purpose?

_____

_____

_____

Is there a *what* you need to let go of? What is it?

_____

_____

Step 4: Define Done

Review your map from Step 2 with the green-yellow-red designations from Step 3. Locate the clusters of nonalignment (yellow and red) and focus in on the top level identity that doesn't align with your purpose.

Use the template on the next page to assess this top level identity. Dream big when you think about what alignment could look like. Don't shortchange yourself or settle for less, really focus in on true alignment. *Shed the should* as you work through this process.

Once you have completed the assessment of the top level identity, review which identities still need alignment defined and address the next highest level. Use one template for each assessment. You can print more from my website, if needed. It's also included in the Template Appendix.

Defining Done

Cluster Top Level Identity Name _____

Dream Big – What does alignment at this top level look like?

_____

_____

_____

_____

How does aligning this top level identity trickle down through the cluster?

_____

_____

_____

What lower level identities still need to be addressed?

_____

_____

_____

Defining Done

Cluster Top Level Identity Name _____

Dream Big – What does alignment at this top level look like?

_____

_____

_____

_____

_____

How does aligning this top level identity trickle down through the cluster?

_____

_____

_____

What lower level identities still need to be addressed?

_____

_____

_____

Defining Done

Cluster Top Level Identity Name _____

Dream Big – What does alignment at this top level look like?

_____

_____

_____

_____

How does aligning this top level identity trickle down through the cluster?

_____

_____

_____

What lower level identities still need to be addressed?

_____

_____

Defining Done

Cluster Top Level Identity Name _____

Dream Big – What does alignment at this top level look like?

_____

_____

_____

_____

_____

How does aligning this top level identity trickle down through the cluster?

_____

_____

_____

What lower level identities still need to be addressed?

_____

_____

_____

Step 5: Plot Your Course

One by one, review the identities that you identified as needing change to bring alignment in Step 4.

Use the template on the next two pages to understand what change needs to happen to bring about that alignment. Plot out decisions, steps, and dependencies for this change. If you need more copies, you can find the template in the Template Appendix.

It can be big! Steps break big jobs down so you can make incremental progress without being overwhelmed. There's joy and relief in incremental progress, too.

Remember that your lodestar is your purpose. Evaluate your choices against that purpose. Is your decision in alignment as well as the eventual result? What about the actions you will need to take? Are they in alignment?

Tap into your gardening toolbox, especially including your village, if you find you need some clarity with this step.

Plotting Your Course

Identity Name _____

Current State Summary

_____

_____

Goal State Summary

_____

_____

What needs to change?

_____

_____

What barriers are there to achieving this change today?

_____

_____

_____

What choices do you need to make to achieve this change?

_____

_____

_____

_____

_____

What steps can you take to achieve this change?

_____

_____

_____

_____

_____

Are any of your steps dependent on other steps being done?

_____

_____

_____

_____

_____

Plotting Your Course

Identity Name _____

Current State Summary

_____

_____

Goal State Summary

_____

_____

What needs to change?

_____

_____

_____

What barriers are there to achieving this change today?

_____

_____

_____

What choices do you need to make to achieve this change?

_____

_____

_____

_____

What steps can you take to achieve this change?

_____

_____

_____

_____

Are any of your steps dependent on other steps being done?

_____

_____

_____

_____

Plotting Your Course

Identity Name _____

Current State Summary

_____

_____

Goal State Summary

_____

_____

What needs to change?

_____

_____

_____

What barriers are there to achieving this change today?

_____

_____

_____

What choices do you need to make to achieve this change?

_____

_____

_____

_____

_____

What steps can you take to achieve this change?

_____

_____

_____

_____

Are any of your steps dependent on other steps being done?

_____

_____

_____

_____

Creating and reinforcing a ritual when you are in a strong and firm place gives you an easy entry to this meditative space when you start responding to the world in an emotional way because your brain is fatigued.

Exercise 13: Rituals Are Not Luxuries

In the table below, note different ways you can engage each of your senses. These will become the actions that begin your rituals. Take one or two actions that feel comfortable and natural to you and do them every time you sit down in your personal space to review your map.

Taste	
Touch	
Smell	
Sight	
Sound	

Template Appendix

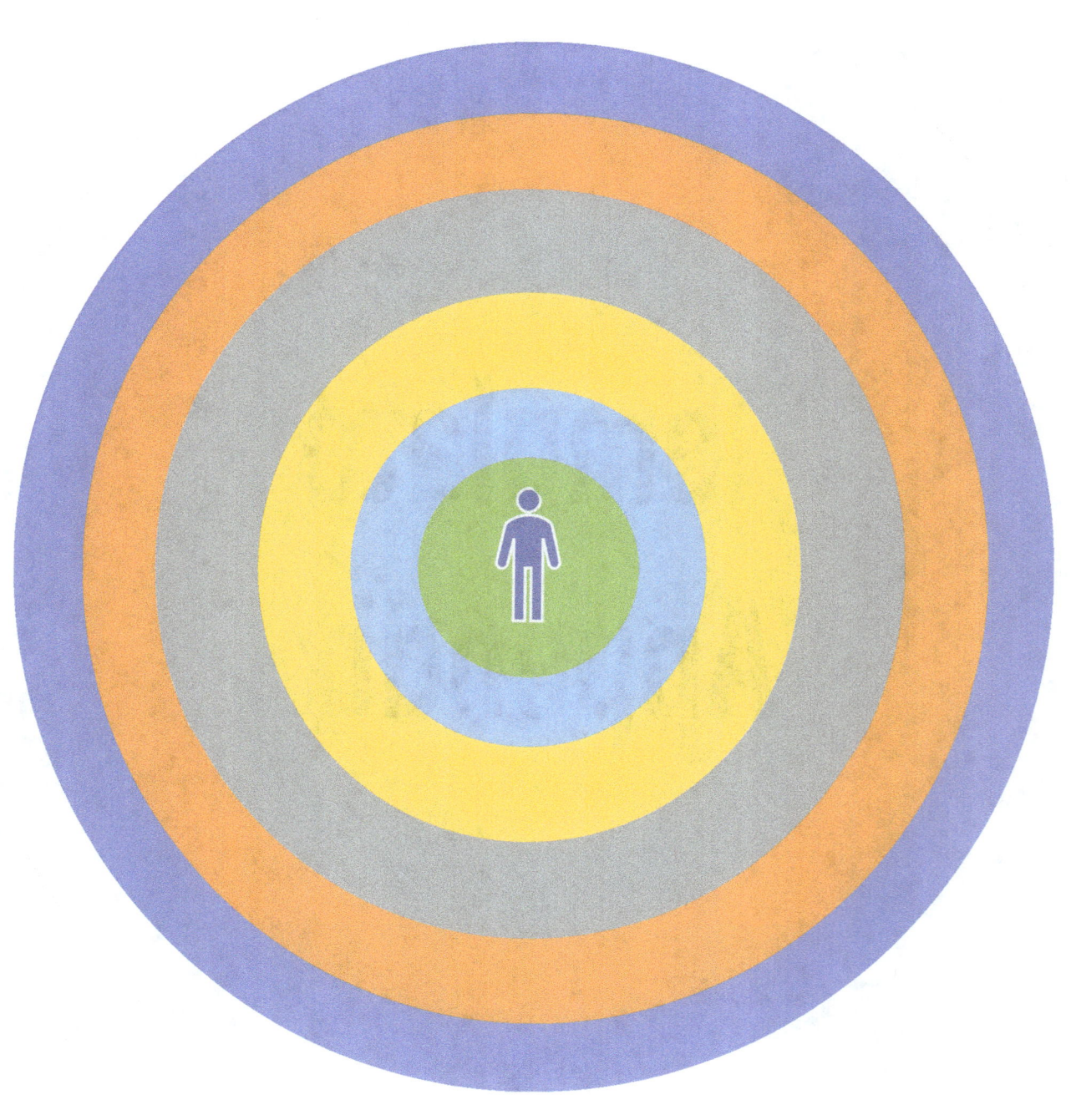

Artifact No.	Description	Words/Ideas	Values

Artifact Description   **Artifact No.** _____

_____

_____

_____

Is this artifact connected to a person, event, or both? Describe the significance of this below.

_____

_____

What emotions are tied to the artifact itself?

_____

_____

What emotions are tied to the people or events connected to this artifact?

_____

_____

What two words/ideas come to mind first when you think about this artifact in totality?

_____

_____

Learned Identity Name	Primary Environment	Interacts with (People)	Restricted in:		
			Behavior?	Language?	Dress?

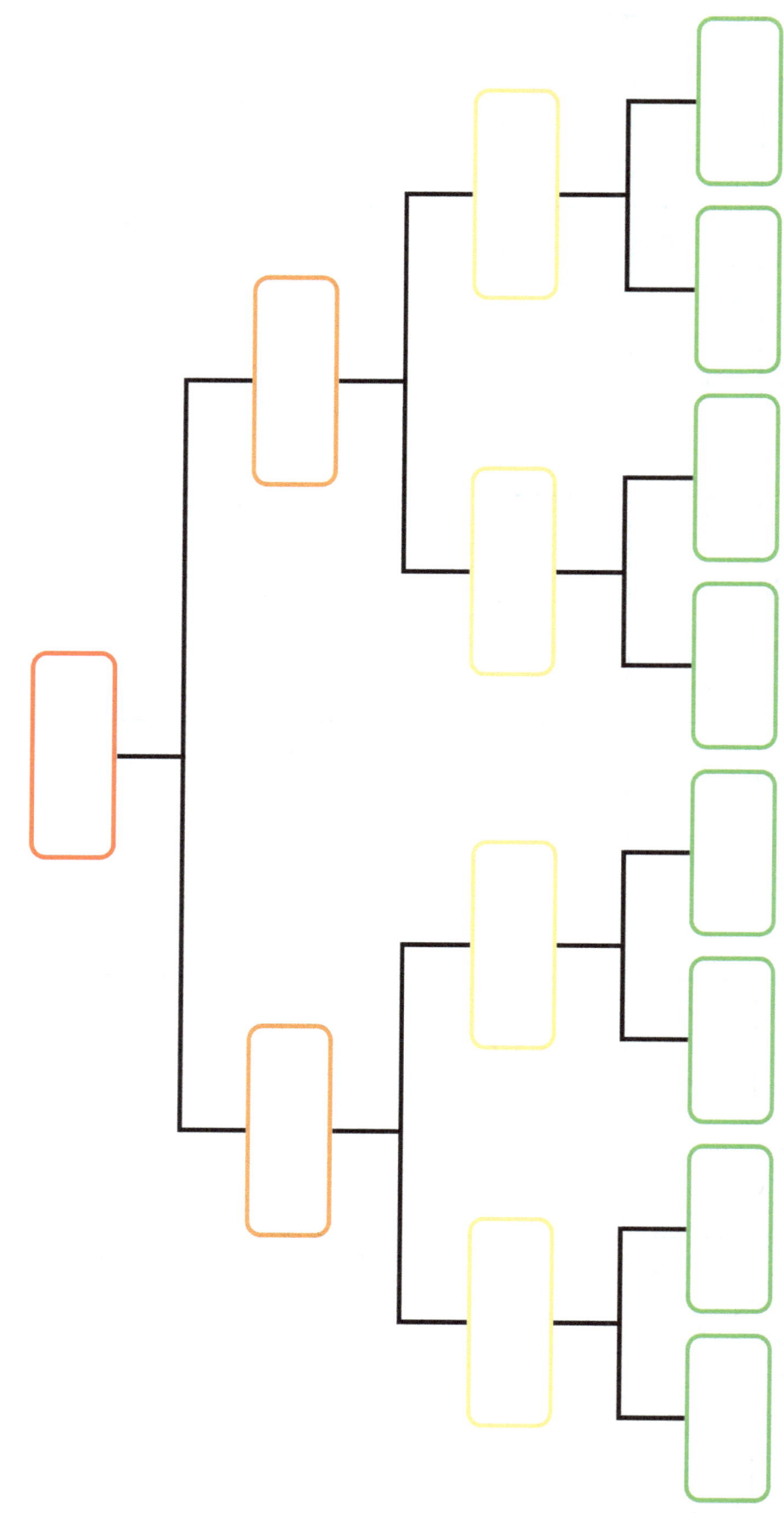

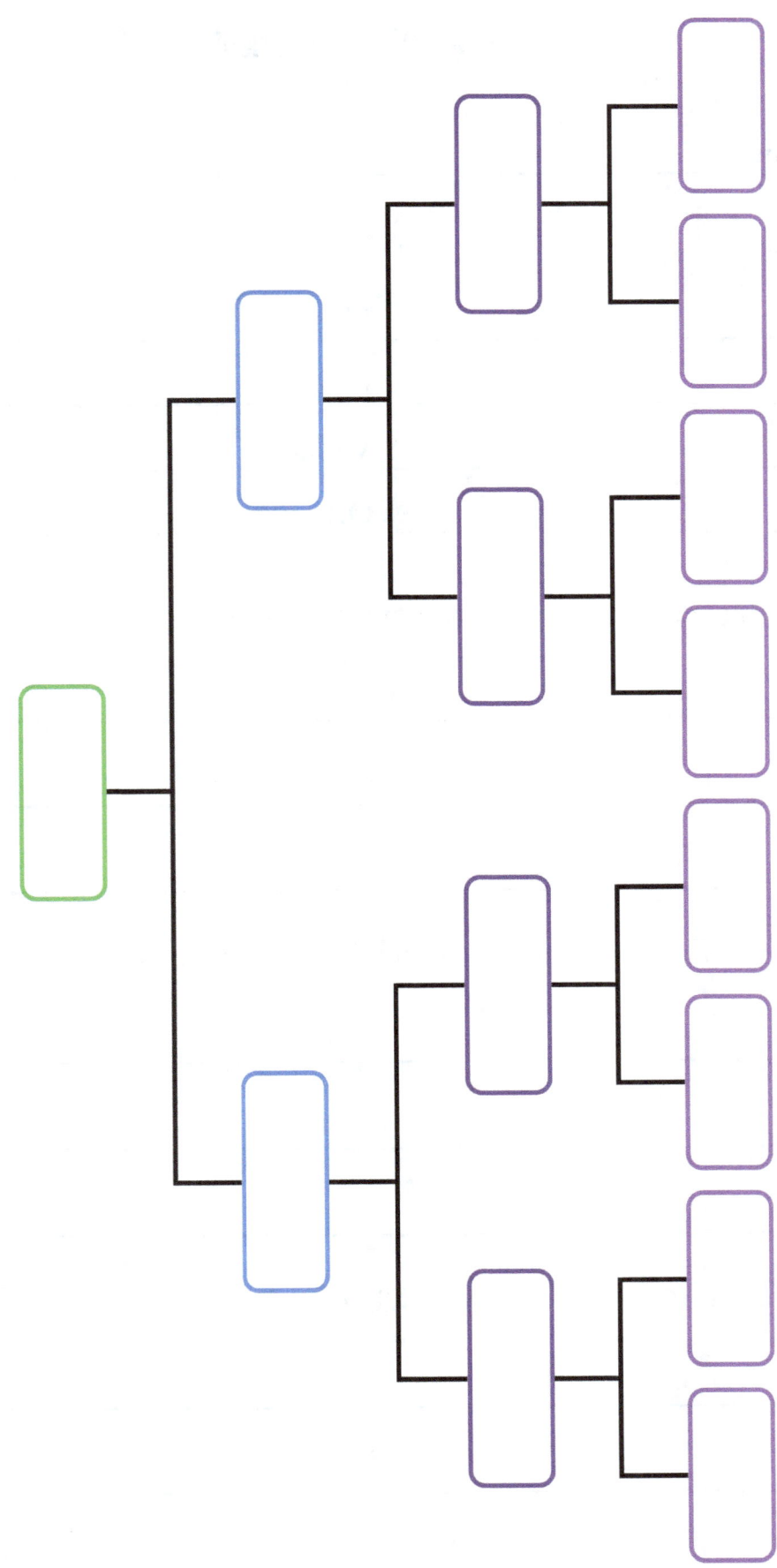

Learned Identity Assessment

Identity Name _____

Identity Path

Red: _____   Blue: _____

Orange: _____   Indigo: _____

Yellow: _____   Violet: _____

Green: _____   Other: _____

What about this identity aligns with your purpose?

_____

_____

_____

What about this identity does not align with your purpose?

_____

_____

_____

Is there a *what* you need to let go of? What is it?

_____

_____

Defining Done

Cluster Top Level Identity Name _____

Dream Big – What does alignment at this top level look like?

_____

_____

_____

_____

How does aligning this top level identity trickle down through the cluster?

_____

_____

_____

What lower level identities still need to be addressed?

_____

_____

_____

Plotting Your Course

Identity Name _____

Current State Summary

_____

_____

Goal State Summary

_____

_____

What needs to change?

_____

_____

_____

What barriers are there to achieving this change today?

_____

_____

_____

_____

What choices do you need to make to achieve this change?

_____

_____

_____

_____

What steps can you take to achieve this change?

_____

_____

_____

_____

Are any of your steps dependent on other steps being done?

_____

_____

_____

_____

Rebecca Claeys is a wisdom steward and purpose coach helping professional women and gender nonconforming people experiencing personal friction claim peace and fulfillment in their lives. She is the creator of the Soul Alchemy Cycle and founder of Cleopatra's Seeds.

Rebecca is a Bachelor's educated Registered Nurse and holds credentials as a Certified Professional Coder and a Certified Program Integrity Professional. She has received numerous accolades for her work during the COVID-19 public health emergency, including a Certificate of Recognition and a Challenge Coin from the State of Wisconsin Department of Health Services and a Certificate of Appreciation from the US Army 78th Training Division.

After running on the corporate hamster wheel for 20 years chasing the next big career step (what she calls 'a what'), Rebecca now helps women and gender nonconforming professionals facing burnout to reclaim their root purpose (what she refers to as 'a why') so they define their freedom, joy, and success on their terms. Connect with her at www.CleopatrasSeeds.com.